What if you had to vacate the premises?

I0101751

Would Family and friends be more likely to take you in if you were prepared?

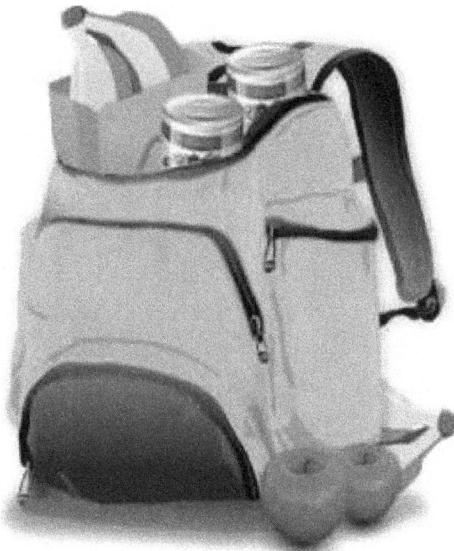

Solar Powered A/C

What if the Trunk of your car was packed with basic food essentials?

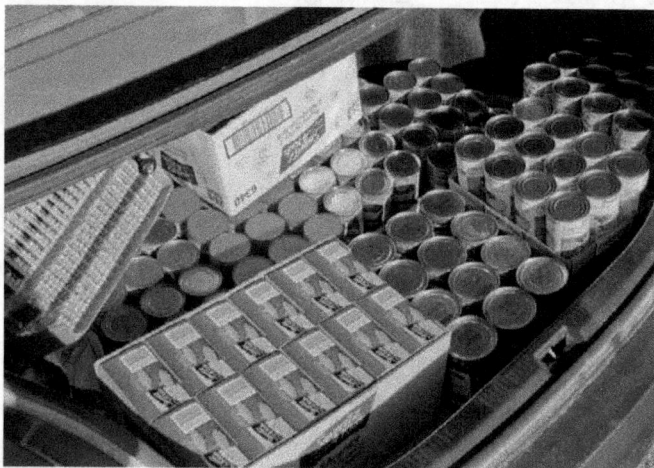

Emergency Prepping City and Suburban Home & Apartments

This book is dedicated to the experiences with mega storms that hit the State of Florida. With power going out in the 95-degree heat, gasoline stations closed or no power, supermarket and grocery stores closed with no power all frozen food trashed and not sellable for liability concerns shelves were empty.

Electricity was spotty at best mostly due to downed overgrown trees and backyard easement access for utility trucks could not access damage lines with sheds, fences and other abstractions in the utility easement area of properties kept the delays going longer.

I decided to put a simple plan in place to have enough food water and the ability to do basic cooking if we had to stay home for minimum of 7-10 day with-ought having to leave during the emergency. A prolonged storm that affected the electric grid with no power till the storm is over and after who knows the time timetable for repairs.

Solar flair activity affects the global weather system, satellite communications & the electric grid our modern conveniences can become temporarily disrupted

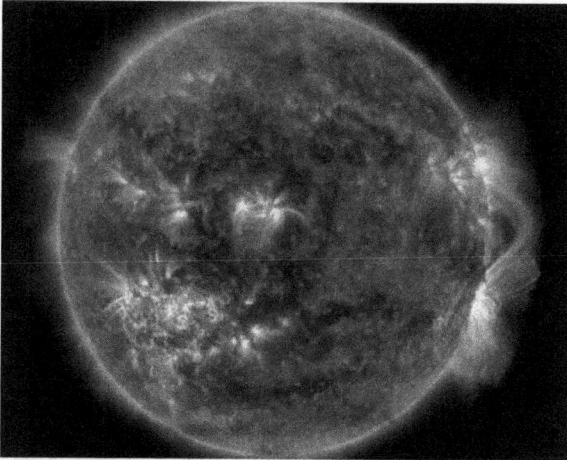

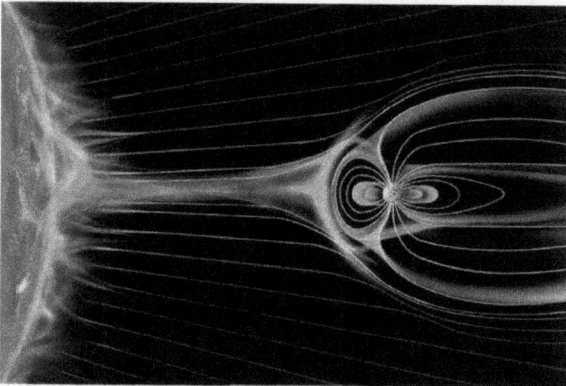

Cooler Bags
Easy to store and ready to use.
They fold and take up little space

Refrigeration may not be available these quick at the ready cooler bags are great to fill with ice in case power goes out. Low cast and space savers for storage.

Disclaimer

Please note the information contained within this document is for educational purposes only.

Every attempt has been made to provide accurate, up to date and reliable complete information no warranties of any kind are expressed or implied. Readers acknowledge that the author is not engaging in rendering legal, financial, Medical or professional advice.

By reading any document, the reader agrees that under no circumstances are we responsible for any losses, direct or indirect that are incurred as a result of use of the information contained within this document including - but not limited to errors, omissions, or inaccuracies.

Prepping for short term Emergencies

This book is for the purpose of providing the reader options of being at the ready in case of hurricane, flooding, severe storms and other problems that may crash the Electric Grid is down and you will not have access to societies services.

Food, Water, Communications you must prepare resources to be able to hold up at your location for days during and possible many days after the storm

Avoid the wait with minimal preparation for 3-7 days you can maintain one backpack of supplies for each person in the household so to avoid the aftermath madness and scramble for resources.

Great organizations like the American Red Cross. (They are the first on the scene in all emergencies all over the World). The Salvation Army is Runner up in Emergency assistance plus local churches of all denominations. Eventually F.E.M.A, State and Emergency authorities after they get done fighting over jurisdiction and protocol paperwork in triplicate.

Katrina in New Orleans, Mississippi and Sandy in the NY, NJ. Just to name a few. Help takes time and Bureaucracies have limited flexibility.

The Overview of Contents:

The Plan
Travel Pack
Hydration Water Filters
Avoid Empty Super Market Selves
Simple Common Food
Food Supplies In Stock worksheet
Children & Separation
Pets
The Elderly
Cooking Options
Funding Cash, Gold & Bartering
Utility Multi Tools, Power tools
Lighting Options Flash Lights LED. etc
Oil Lamps & Candles
Emergency Radio
First Aid Kit, Medications…
Solar Powered A/D Systems
Solar Powered Refrigerator
Solar Powered Freezer
Solar Powered Air conditioning
Portable Power battery backup & Inverters
Portable Solar Power
Solar Powered Freezer and Refrigerator
Evacuation Routs and Maps
Shelter Locations & Worksheet
Sleeping Bags & Air Mattresses

RV, Campers & Tents
Rain Gear
Tarps & Roof Shingles
Safe or Reinforced More Secure Rooms
Gasoline & Gas Generators
Traffic & Delays when to evacuate
Self Protection readiness
Files, Documents and Family Photos
Fishing
Tree Pruning options
Weapon Lockers
Utility Blower Fan
Safe rooms
Outdoor Pyramid all steel structure
Tents
Campers and Motor Homes
Air Mattresses
Sleeping bags and full body sleeping bags
Battery backup and Emergency Car Starter
Battery powered Digital Emergency TV
Power Tools at the ready
Window protection options

The Electric Grid

Since the 1990's America's Electric Grid has been in decline, the only option is to reduce the dependency on centrally manage electric power. By using solar enabled energy for, Cars, Lighting, Refrigerators, Freezers, A/C cooling, etc.

2016 The United States will start a Solar boom due to the expensive cost of energy, and after a few years or shortly after 2020 the sun will be taxed base on the amount of solar energy you collect with your micro solar grid. US Cities have already stopped officering tax deductions because of the reduction of grid taxable revenues are down in significant numbers.

Inside you fill fined a variety of Solar Enhance products to limit the dependency of the Central Power Grid

The Plan

Have a plan with family, Friends in your area
that if one area is affected that you will join forces
by salvaging all you can before you are force by
the emergency or the Authorities to vacate your
home

Hotels and Motels are always booked and are
very expensive in emergencies and you will most
likely be stuck

Rental cars are not easy to get and very expensive

Team up with friend and with preparation of
resources you will not be a burden but and
addition of recourses of food, protection and
support to the group.

Neighbor Plan

When things settle down first thing is to walk the
block your home is on help those who may be
hurt and gather the team or group in your
neighborhood for assisting others and keep a
look out for vandals or bandits who my see your
neighborhood as a opportunity.

Travel Pack
(Bug out Pack)

Each member of you household including the
children should have their travel pack
With each combination of emergency supplies in
case they are separated by necessity

Water is the Most Essential in emergency (Commodity)

When you do not have to Vacate

Smaller bottles for travel

Water Filter (Commodity)

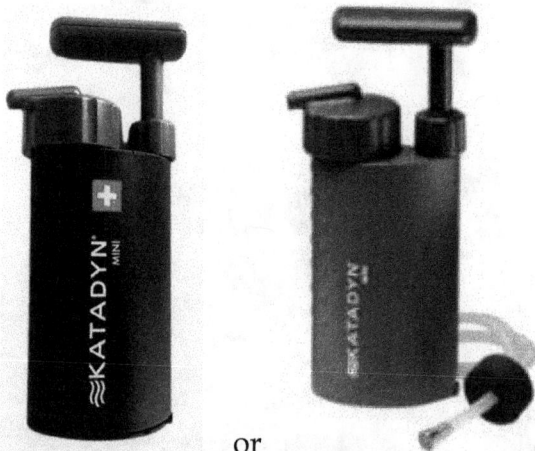

or

Light weight and compact, yet high purifying capability water purifier, which is used, all over the world.

Personal pump water filters which is one of the lightest and most compact water filter units available on the entire market. It is ideal for hiking, camping, hunting, fishing, bicycling, travel, business trips, and other uses. filtersfast.com

Super Market Selves
Just before a storm

During any or even the possibility of
an incoming storm?

People will buy out everything on the
selves weather they need it or not

It takes several days or weeks for
the distribution networks to replenish
the entire variety of the supermarket
selves and if people have been
displace from the area much longer.

Supply Chain Distribution

People evacuate, equipment Damage, Business just get wiped out. Insurance takes weeks or months to process in normal times. Employees leave the area

Rebuilding becomes a Process of strength

AnthonyKovic.com or Connect Anthony@AnthonyKovic.com

Old Land line Phones

They may still work on older networks but the newer land line phones are Internet or I.P. based, they my look like a land line connected to your phone jack but require power from you home to work

Check if you have a phone router box in your basement or garage your home phone may need a power source it may also have a battery backup call your phone company for details

Soups
(Commodity)

Hearty, Fast and come with its own
Liquid source
Multi Year expiration date
Ready to Eat Just Open
self opening
Can and can be eaten
Cold or warm up for better taste

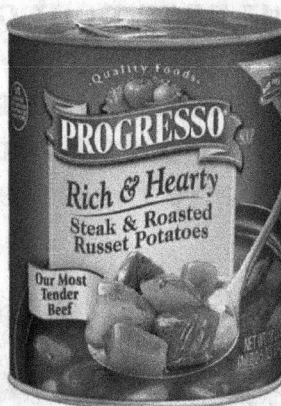

You can have enough soup for each
person stored in a pantry, closet or
just under the bed for up to 2 years
or more shelf life (best rotate every
6 months to 1 year)

Power Bars (Commodity)

Easy to store and carry Portable food with long self-life.

Power bars or the equivalent have a long self-life great for backpack stuffing and if you need to be on the move Easy to share and great for trading!

Meat
Beef Jerky
(Commodity)

Many varieties with great self life for on the go food and snacking a backpack stuffer. This is great for trading

Food Supplies
In Stock - Location

_____ - _____

_____ - _____

_____ - _____

_____ - _____

_____ - _____

_____ - _____

_____ - _____

_____ - _____

_____ - _____

_____ - _____

_____ - _____

_____ - _____

_____ - _____

_____ - _____

Small Frying Pan
Is a Must for cooking and should be a part of the travel kit

Cooking Soup, Eggs, beacon etc.

A Small Souse pan is vital for quick soup or stew warm up for an entire group the soap cans are 16 oz's and 2 cans can be great for 3-4 people as a quick lunch.

Ice & Cooler
Placing water bottles in freezer keeps food Cold in Cooler when power goes out

Solar Refrigerating & Freezing
The Technology is here Look for it

Solar Technology for On or Off the Grid

AnthonyKovic.com or Connect Anthony@AnthonyKovic.com

Illuminating Solar Blinds

10 am 4 pm 7 pm

9 pm 10 pm 11 pm

Toilet Paper (Commodity)
Should not be taken lightly

Keeping a few 5 Gallon Bottles filled with Tap water can be a lifesaver for the toilet with No Running water is available. Plus it is a great supply of fresh water if needed

Whistle

A must have tool for communications or if lost. The human voice can yell only so much before you loose your voice.

A great whistle can be blown for a long time and the sound will carry a longer distance with little effort

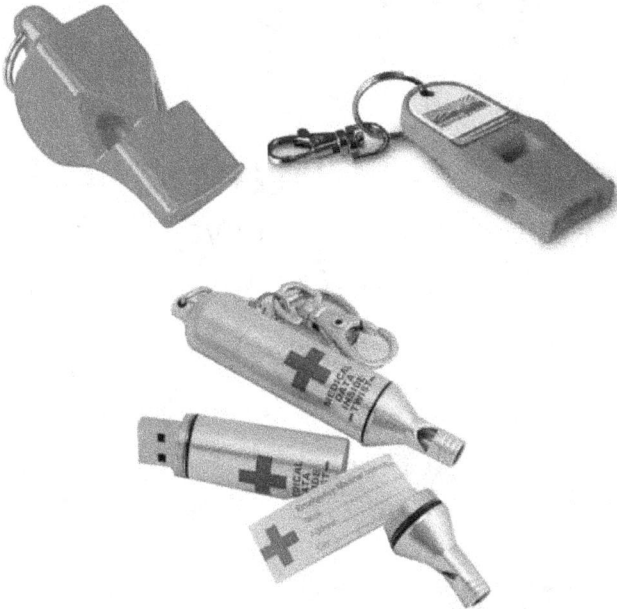

USB First Medical Info Whistle Carry your Health Data if relocation is required

Glass Breaker

With Storm water rising, roadways
can be covered and hiding deep
water or driving off road into a lake

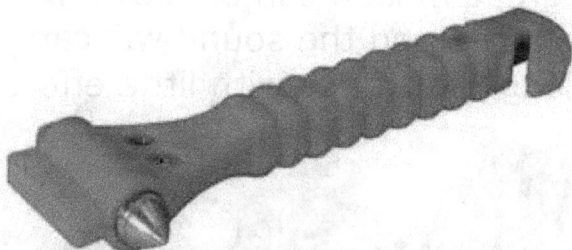

Seat Belt Cutter Combo

A must have if you live in active
flood zone areas during storms

Air Horn

A communications tool to Help alert others something is happening in your area when phones are not working

Window Storm protection

Window Strom shutters

Manual or Motorized Options
Storm shutters

Reinforced window Film

Window Film easy and quick to apply

Separation

If needing to separate from the group and no communications is available.

1. Leave word with People you have made plans to communicate with.

2. After a period of time a specific meeting places.

3. Phone messages can be accessed from remote emergency phones

4. Voice messages: one can connect or have emergency phone access from another persons phone

Meet at a designated hotel or motel you can leave word at the front desk if you have to leave.

If Separated
Meeting Locations

Day 1 - Location

_____-_____

Day 2 - Location

_____-_____

Day 3 - People to Call

_____#_____

_____#_____

_____#_____

_____#_____

_____#_____

Locations and People you will leave
word of your location you will be
going or Traveling to Shelters etc.
They will have Name List of those
who are at that location.

Children

Special food, Snacks, Toys
Keeping them calm in emergency

When you or other members of the
family or group are in panic
The children will be afraid and
exacerbate the tension with crying

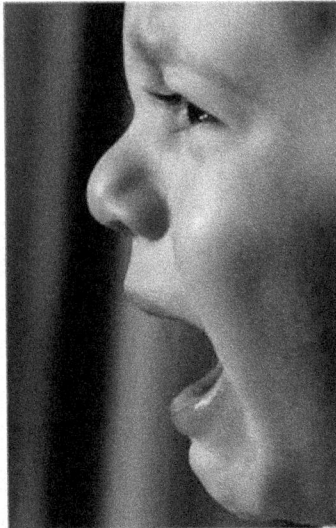

Medicines and other medical needs
should be ready in advance with an
approaching storm

Elderly
Family Members

The Elderly Family members either
at home or a specific location their
needs and supplies should be
prepared in advance in case you had
to pick them up to bring to your
location so they are ready to travel

Solar Powered A/C

12000 BTU Ductless Split Air Conditioner
Cool & Heat SEER Up to 28

Cooking Stove (Sterno)
(Follow Product Label Instructions)

Sterno Pop Up Stove Easy to use

Sterno Fuel: Long Lasting
Will heat up 16 oz can of soup in
5-7minutes in a small pan. Soup is
ready to eat in minutes
Portable easy to take with you

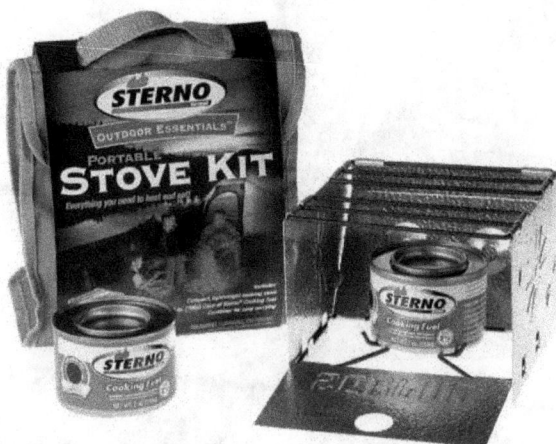

3 or more Sterno Stoves in stock
Have at least 10 Cans of the 2 Hour
Sterno Fuel in stock And 10 Cans of
the Sterno 45 Minute fuel in stock
in case people need to split up

Lighters – Matches (Commodity)

Each backpack should have 2-3 lighters
Clear Lighters so you know fuel is in them

Charcoal Grill
Tabletop grills for outdoor use only
(Follow Product Label Instructions)

Gas Grill

Small gas grill for outdoors use area homes or apartments with a balcony or patio works great for outside barbeque cooking

Butane stove
Simple Inexpensive
(Follow Product Label Instructions)

Simple cost affective for emergency these units are portable and some manufacturers have a custom carry case

Sugar
(Commodity)

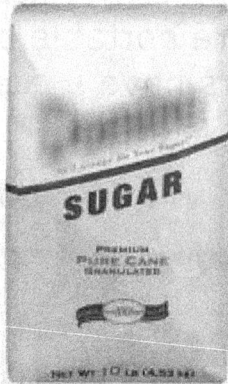

It also has the value of money
People need to eat drink tea coffee

Keep in Airtight containers to protect
it from Contamination

Alcohol
(Commodity)

Many uses other than for drinking
such disinfectant

Look for lowest cost to keep in stock
long self-file and best if it is in plastic
bottles if possible to keep from
accidental breakage

Cash
In Power Failure
ATM and Banks may Not
be working or have any $$ left

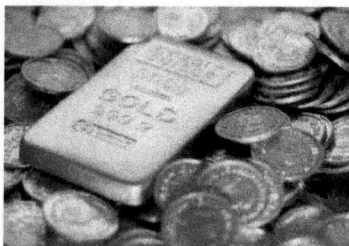

In short time Emergencies Gold is not easy to make change for a bottle of water or a can of soup.

Utility Multi Tool

For that quick fix, this all around tool
is great for those living in Cities or
Apartment or if you had to vacate
your home and need to open a can
of food etc.

Power tools
Charge all your batteries for emergency use

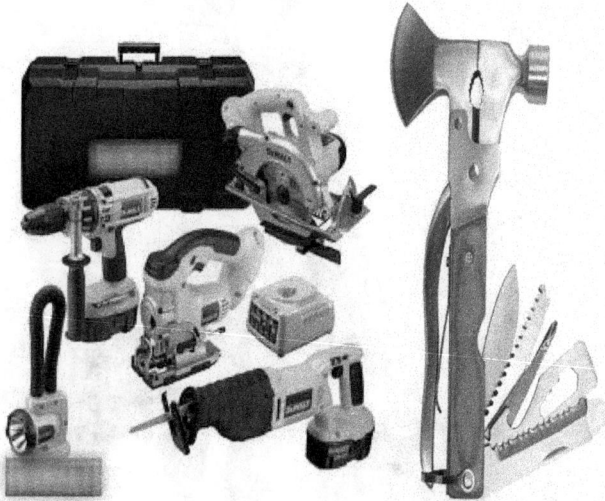

Quick Minor Repairs can keep the damage from spreading and becoming a large problem

Solar Powered Battery Chargers will keep the repairs going

Tarps
(Commodity)

A few tarps can be useful in roof leaks to keep small leaks from becoming bigger

Best used with proper Roofing nails
www.tarpfactoryoutlet.com

Roof Shingles

Loose Roof Shingles can be repaired
with Roof Cement tube before the
storm so wind does not destroy them

Having a small supply of your tiles
before the storm will be a roof saver
because they will be sold out quickly

Have a Local Roofer provide you with options

LED Flash Light

Longer lasting LED lights with
Batteries of AA Size are the most
popular Have several similar
Flashlight with same battery size

(Commodity)

Buy them in 100 AA Pack
Check Date for Shelf life
They sell out quickly before a storm

Wall Mounted Oil lamp
(Commodity)

This Oil Lamp is always at the ready
On the wall + it is portable if needed

(Follow Label for Cautions)

- One 22 Oz of these bottle will provide
  Light for 6-10 or more Hours
- Get to know the Lamp Properly setup the
  Wick so it burns the Oil not the Wick

Battery Powered LED Lanterns

They are the best option

Best to purchase lighting products with one battery size if possible and purchase them in bulk

Candles
(Commodity)

(Follow Manufacture Label for Cautions)
Candles are a Fire Hazard and should
be placed in stable protective casing,
if tipped over will not create a fire

Candles for emergency light, each
candle burns for 5 hours!!!

Decorative Candle Holders

Many Styles of candleholders with wall mounting options can provide beauty style and emergency lighting when needed

Citronella candle helps repel mosquitoes; candle burns for up to 40 hrs

Emergency Radio (Commodity)

Radio, Light, Crank Power, Cell Phone Charger Many models available but check all its factions work especially the Crank Charging ability

Cranking charger can charge both the unit and a variety of cell phones for added power when you need it.

Digital TV
Battery Powered
A source for entertainment and
Emergency use

Runs on AA
Batteries

First Aid Kit (Commodity)

Basic Kit is must for every home

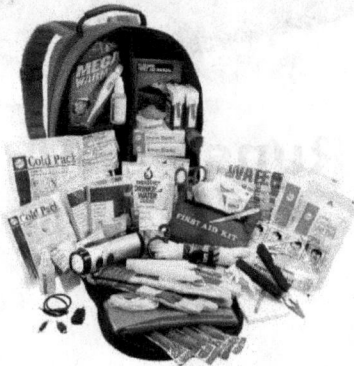

Medications (Commodity)

Keep a List of Medications
Most National Pharmacies chains
May have and can fill your prescription at any
Location with refills left on file

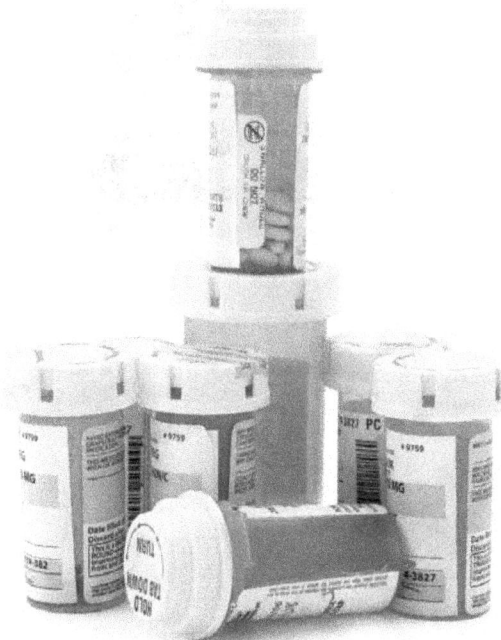

Portable Power
Battery Backups & Inverters
With small 300 watt to 1,500 or more

A Lamp with a Low wattage LED Table Lamp
Light up a room, great with CFC or Led bulbs
Keep your Cell phone charged

- Runs 115-volt AC or 12-volt DC products anywhere Built-in 400 watt inverter

- Sealed, non-spillable 20 amp-hour AGM battery

- 250 PSI Air compressor for inflating tires and small sports equipment

- Jumper cables designed for safe and efficient jump-starting

- Built-in light provides illumination in emergency situations at home and on the road

- 3-digit display allows for easy battery status monitoring

- Audible alarm signals overheat and under voltage conditions

- Overload and over-temperature protection to ensure longer inverter life

- AC charger stored in the unit

- Recharge at home or from a vehicle

Car Inverter
3 Power Options Unit

Great for changing phone, PDA, Laptop Cell phone and other items in the 75-100 watt range.

More Powerful Inverters are available

Portable Solar Power (Commodity)

Solar power units such as this one is coming to retail made for reducing your energy costs by charging low powered technology like phones, tablet computers etc.

They are a great source of continuous power when the Electric Grid is Down and can be use in apartment buildings with enough sun coming thru a window or access to patio to catch the direct sun light.

Evacuation Routes & Maps

Map Out your Evacuation Routes in your area and where they take you to pre-planned places you have done research on and advise family and friends of route and destination

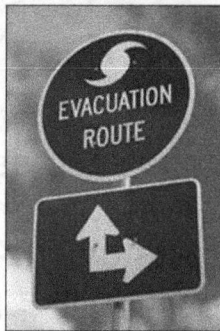

Evacuate or stay? There are two paths. Which path should you take?

Contact your local emergency management office to find your evacuation route and guides are available at government offices or search the Internet for your area evacuation routes

Shelter Locations

Contact your local emergency management office to find your local shelter Locations. Note they change from Emergency to Emergency pay attention to local programming for these updates or call the local Police or Sheriff's office. The fill up quickly

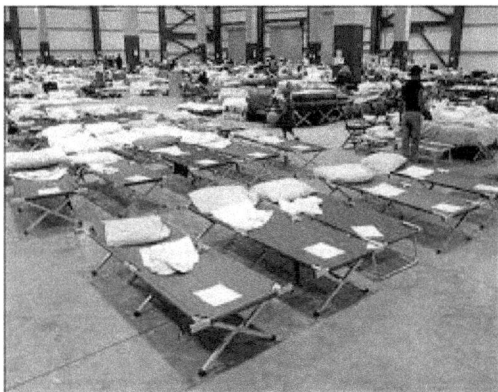

What should you bring with you to the emergency shelter? Call ahead of the storms for more info

Shelter – Locations
Keep a list of the most used Shelter Locations

—

_____ — _____

—

_____ — _____

—

_____ — _____

—

_____ — _____

—

_____ — _____

—

_____ — _____

—

_____ — _____

—

_____ — _____

—

_____ — _____

—

_____ — _____

—

_____ — _____

—

_____ — _____

Sleeping Bags

They can come in handy if you had
to vacate to family and friends

These sleeping bags require no
bedding and you can easily sleep on
the couch or on the road.

Most sleeping bags can be low cost
and take up little space when rolled
up in its carrying case.

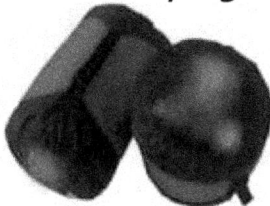

Air Mattress

Air Mattresses can come in handy it is best to have individual air mattresses. You may be in a place that does not have large areas of open space to put in a Queen or King size mattress. You may have to inflate and deflate daily with no electricity

Best to have a foot pub backup

Flatbed truck air mattress

Even a pool Mattress can be more comfortable than the floor and easy to inflate to seep on

RV or Camper

Making arrangements for the RV to be parked a distance from your home or leave the area entirely before the storm may be the best option before the roads are closed.

Anchor your camper down
See Manufacture Label for best securing your camper or motor home or tent

Tent

Camping is an option
Porch or backyard area of the
Property or a Campsite

A tent with access to bathroom and
shower is only temporary option

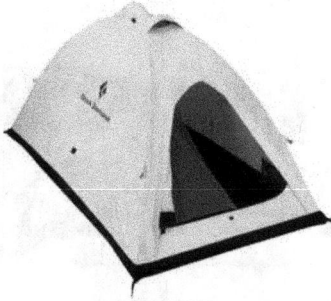

You may have Camp on your own
property while repairs take place

Rain & Gear

Portable Rain Suite (Stay protected
from the elements is a # 1 priority)

You May have to get out to fix a flat
tire in wind and rain if you get all
wet may not be able to get dry for
hours in cold wet clothing

Safe Room
Closet or bathroom modified so it would be stronger and better Protected from debris with Solid reinforced walls

Portable Safe room or built into a functional Closet space

Contractors are adding them as options for new construction Or a closet could be build with Concrete or Cinder blocks with heavy Door

Outdoor Hurricane Pyramid
All steel structure

Portable
Outdoor options with a heavy steel
frame and skin

Simple for above ground when digging is not an
option from high water table

Pets
The family pets
Can they be protected?

What if you cannot bring them
along?

Is it more humane to set the loose or
to trap them in the home with loose
food and water?

Some battery powered food
dispensers can provide food for
several days or even a week

When traveling you pet may want the favorite
sleeping bag when in a new location

AnthonyKovic.com or Connect Anthony@AnthonyKovic.com

Utility Fan

Utility fan/Blower have a large air flow
output, which creates a sizable breeze

When A/C not available and you need air
flow and a fan blower great option

Gasoline
(Commodity)
(Follow Container Label Cautions)
Gas should be in proper containers in a secure area

Small Gasoline generators require fresh clean fuel

Fuel stabilizer will keep your fuel fresh for a longer period of time. Old fuel will destroy your engine and will make your emergency a bigger one.

Traffic & Delays

Evacuation areas the traffic can be very heavy. Being ready early can increase your exit time.

Most delays are coursed by out of gas cars on the roadways you could be in traffic for many hours in bad weather.   Have Alternate options ready with maps and routes planned out and call ahead to secure reservations.

Gas Generators
(Follow User Instructions provided by Manufacturer)
(Commodity)

You should be an expert in its use and maintained properly or they will not work when you need it

Fresh fuel is essential; the tiny carburetor will clog quickly with any impurities in the fuel.

Self Protection
Fallow All Laws
(Commodity)

When Natural disasters such as a hurricanes come thru an area cities are most vulnerable, as we have seen in New Orleans.

Safety in groups with experienced law enforcement family and friends looking out for each other

The Revolver is more reliable and simpler to maintain in working condition than the more complex stylish self-defense options

Trigger locks come in Key and Combination Options for easy access.

Ammunition
Follow all Laws

Ammunition is a valuable trading currency

Ammunition size can determine quantity and availability a the store

Gun Safety locks for all Guns

All Weapons can be secured with trigger & other security locks to keep secured from children and others from misusing them

Hunting
For food may be an option
Hunting season in your area may be open (Check licensing in the area)

Weapon Lockers

Trigger locks and other weapon security devices are added to protect people from misusing weapons by keeping them lock.

Fishing
A small tackle box
or just a compact rod and real

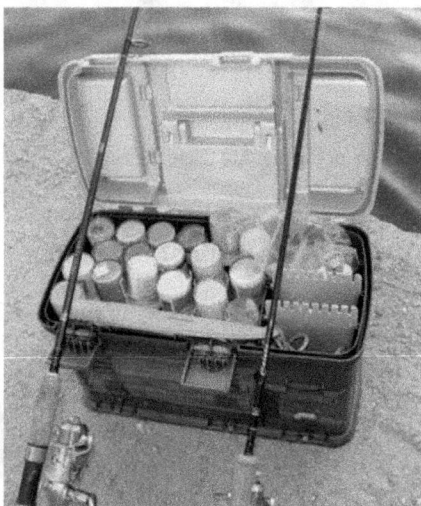

Tree Pruning
Call for Utility Pruning
It is everyone's Responsibility to notify the Utility of a hazardous tree. In many cases you do not have to own the property to call for a utility pruning, it is their responsibility to keep the trees pruned to avoid power line damage and outages

Utility Pruning

Right Tree Right Place

If you see an overgrown tree that in a storm will create a hazard to the Utility Lines call it in.

Photos and Files Portability

Most printers have a built in scanner your important files can be scanned and put on the cloud. USB data Drive and the many portable memory chips

In Stock - Location

_____ - _____
_____ - _____
_____ - _____
_____ - _____
_____ - _____
_____ - _____
_____ - _____
_____ - _____
_____ - _____
_____ - _____
_____ - _____
_____ - _____
_____ - _____
_____ - _____
_____ - _____
_____ - _____

Notes

_____

_____

_____

_____

_____

_____

_____

_____

_____

_____

_____

_____

_____

_____

_____

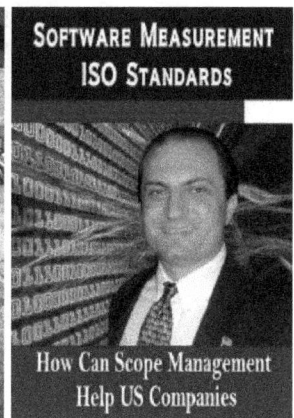

FREE MEMBER ACCESS

Proof of Purchase of any of the tittles on www.AnthonyKovic.com gets you complimentary (One Year) access to Membership training site: www.RealVideoProduction.com

Any Purchase of a book, DVD, Download or rental qualifies as a purchase. Save the emailed receipt sent to you by any participating retailer.

Thank you for your purchase of this or any of our fine products.